CONTENTS

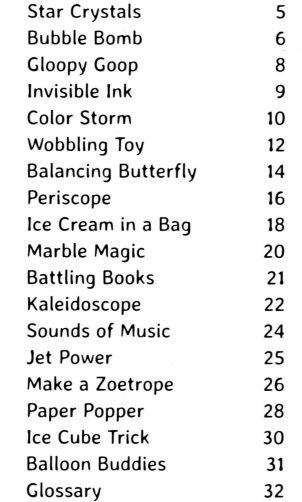

Balloon Kebab	4
Star Crystals	5
Bubble Bomb	6
Gloopy Goop	8
Invisible Ink	9
Color Storm	10
Wobbling Toy	12
Balancing Butterfly	14
Periscope	16
Ice Cream in a Bag	18
Marble Magic	20
Battling Books	21
Kaleidoscope	22
Sounds of Music	24
Jet Power	25
Make a Zoetrope	26
Paper Popper	28
Ice Cube Trick	30
Balloon Buddies	31
Glossary	32
Index	32

BALLOON KABOB

You will need
- Balloons
- A bamboo skewer
- Vegetable oil

Can you put a kabob skewer through a balloon without popping it? If it sounds impossible, think again! Amaze your friends and family by making a balloon kabob.

1

Blow up a balloon to about half its full size, and tie a knot in its neck.

2

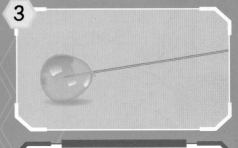

Wipe a little vegetable oil on the skewer. This will help it slide into the balloon smoothly.

3

Poke the point of the skewer into the balloon, near the knot. Push the skewer very gently, twisting as you push.

4

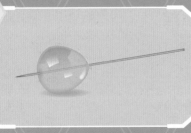

Poke the skewer out on the opposite end of the balloon, through the dark patch.

5

If you have a long skewer, try to add more balloons— like a kabob!

DANGER!

If you poke the balloon in the middle with the skewer, it will **POP!**

What Happens?

Normally, when a balloon is stabbed with a bamboo skewer, the rubber skin will tear, and it will pop. That is because the pressurized air inside the balloon is stretching the skin very tight, so that the slightest hole blows it open in an instant. However, the skin is not as tight at the darker ends of the balloon. So stabbing it there won't pop it—as long as you're careful.

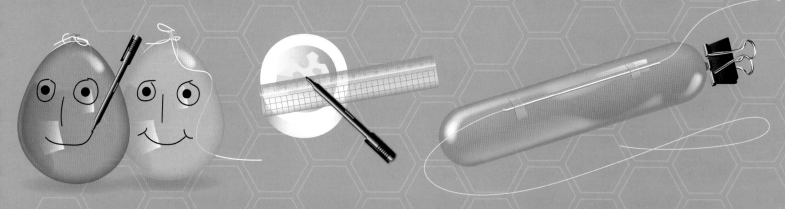

AMAZING
SCIENCE
EXPERIMENTS

ARCTURUS

Having Fun and Being Safe

Inside this book you'll find a whole range of exciting science experiments that can be performed safely at home. The experiments have been designed so that nearly all the equipment you need should be available from around your home. Anything that you don't have at home should be available at a local store.

We would recommend close adult supervision for any experiment involving cooking equipment, sharp implements, electrical equipment, or batteries.

The author and publisher cannot take responsibility for any injury, damage, or mess that might occur as a result of attempting the experiments in this book. Always tell an adult before you perform any experiments, and follow the instructions carefully.

ARCTURUS

This edition published in 2017 by Arcturus Publishing Limited
26/27 Bickels Yard, 151–153 Bermondsey Street,
London SE1 3HA

CH004932US
Supplier 13, Date 0317, Print run 4827

Editors: Joe Harris, Alex Woolf and Joe Fullman
Illustrator: Adam Linley
Designer: Elaine Wilkinson

Printed in China

STAR CRYSTALS

A crystal is a solid material that forms into a regular 3-D pattern. Crystals form when liquid cools, hardens, and turns into a solid. This happens when water is cooled and becomes ice.

You will need
- A glass jar
- Sugar and a tablespoon
- Hot water
- An ice pop stick
- String
- A pipe cleaner

1

Put some hot water into a glass jar. Water from the hot-water faucet should be hot enough.

2

Add sugar, one spoon at a time. Stir with the ice pop stick. Keep adding sugar until you can't dissolve anymore.

3

Make a star shape with a pipe cleaner. Use the string to tie it to the ice pop stick.

4

Hang the star in the sugar solution, resting the stick across the rim of the jar.

5

As the solution cools, crystals begin to form on the star, as long as you've made a saturated solution. But be patient: It can take a few days for crystals to form.

What Happens?

The sugar dissolves in the water to form a sugar solution. Hot water allows more sugar to dissolve. As the water cools, it cannot hold as much sugar in solution, and some sugar changes back to a solid. The arrangement of atoms in the solid produces the shape of the crystal—and these crystals form around the star-shaped pipe cleaner.

BUBBLE BOMB

You will need
- Warm water
- A measuring cup
- A ziplock plastic bag
- A paper towel
- 2 tablespoons of baking soda
- Vinegar

Make a fun and safe "bomb" that will explode with a loud pop! It's best to do this experiment in the bathroom—it might get a little messy!

1

Find a place where you can make a mess, such as in the bathtub. You can also do the experiment outside, in the yard.

2

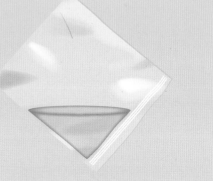

Test your plastic bag for leaks. Put some water in it, close the seal, and turn it over. If no water leaks out, it's good to use.

3

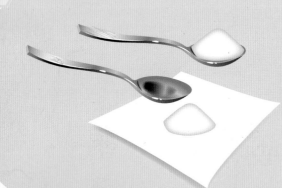

Place your paper towel on a flat surface. Now put 2 tablespoons of baking soda in the center of the square.

4

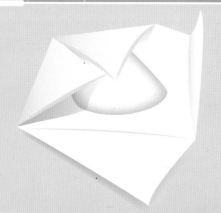

Fold the paper towel into the middle, enclosing the mound of baking soda.

5

Mix together 10 fluid ounces (300 ml) of vinegar and 5 fluid ounces (150 ml) of warm water in the measuring cup.

6

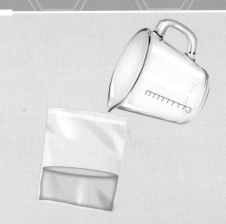

Pour the mixture into the plastic bag, being careful not to spill it on your table.

7

Put the paper towel package into the bag, holding it in the corner away from the liquid while you seal the bag.

8

Shake the bag a little, then place it on the floor or in the bathtub, and stand back. The bag will swell up ...

... and then POP!

What Happens?

Vinegar is an acid and baking soda is a base. When you mix acids and bases together, they react and turn into different chemicals. In this experiment, carbon dioxide gas forms, and there isn't enough room for it in the plastic bag. So the pressure builds up until the bag swells and explodes, releasing the carbon dioxide gas.

GLOOPY GOOP

You will need
- 1 cup of cornstarch
- ½ cup of water
- A mixing bowl
- Food color

Make some strange slime that is not really a liquid—but not really a solid, either! See if you can find out what kind of material it is.

1

Pour a cup of cornstarch into a mixing bowl, and run your fingers through it. It should feel smooth and silky in your hands.

2

Add two drops of food color to ½ cup of water.

3

Mix the water into the cornstarch using your fingers. How does it feel now?

4

Squeeze a handful of the mixture you've made into a ball. It will become a solid!

5

Relax your hand—the mixture will become liquid and run through your fingers!

6

Let the gloop settle in the bowl. Touch the surface gently, then tap it hard.

What Happens?

When this mixture is put under pressure, the cornstarch molecules are forced together, and it behaves like a solid. When it is handled gently, the cornstarch molecules can move around freely, and it flows like a liquid. Quicksand works in just the same way!

INVISIBLE INK

Create a treasure map for your friends using this top secret invisible ink. The combination of lemon juice and heat will help you to reveal your secret mission!

You will need
- A toothpick
- A lemon
- A bowl
- Paper
- Heat source, such as a light bulb or iron

 1

Ask an adult to cut a lemon in half for you. Squeeze the lemon juice into a small bowl.

2

Dip the toothpick into the lemon juice.

3

Use the toothpick to draw your secret map on some paper.

 4

Allow the paper to dry, so that you can't see the drawing anymore.

5

Now warm the paper under a heat source, such as a lamp. As the "ink" gets warm, your secret map is revealed.

What Happens?

Paper is made up of cellulose, or vegetable fibers, from trees. Lemon juice contains an acid that breaks down cellulose and turns it into sugars. When you heat the paper, the heat caramelizes the sugars, making your lemony '"ink" turn brown. Your map is now visible!

COLOR STORM

You will need
- 2 white plates
- Whole milk
- Dishwashing liquid
- 3 or 4 colors of food color
- A notebook and pencil

Oil and water don't mix. Or do they? In fact, milk contains both. This experiment will create colorful patterns with both oil and water.

1

Pour a pool of water into the middle of a white plate, so that it covers the inner hollow.

2

Once the water has settled, put in some evenly spaced drops of food color.

3

Pour some milk into the middle of the other plate.

4

Once the milk has settled, add some drops of different food color, evenly spaced.

5

Carefully add one drop of dishwashing liquid to each of the plates.

6

Make a note of what you see in each plate. You could draw a picture if you like.

7

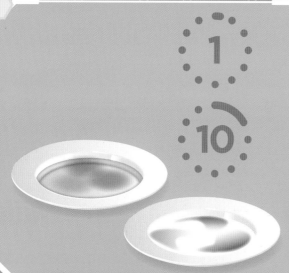

Look at the two plates after 10 minutes and again after 20 minutes. What has changed? Write down the changes that you notice to the liquid.

What Happens?

Milk is a special mixture of fat and water called an emulsion. The fat is not dissolved in the water, but the two are mixed together. The food color doesn't travel through milk as easily as it does through water. This is because it mixes with only the watery part of the milk.

When you add dishwashing liquid, two things happen. First, the surface tension of the water is destroyed. Then, because the dishwashing liquid breaks up the fat, the fat and water start to mix together. The movement of the food color shows you what's happening. It moves to the side of the saucer when the surface tension if broken. And it swirls in patterns as the fat and water start to mix together.

WOBBLING TOY

This wobbling toy refuses to fall down. No matter how hard you knock the toy, it will wobble back up again!

You will need
- A table tennis ball
- Scissors
- A piece of thin cardstock
- A ruler • A pencil
- Colored pens
- Tape • Glue
- Modeling clay

1

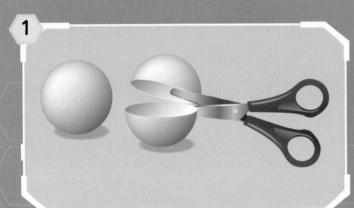

Get an adult to help you cut a table tennis ball in half. It helps to make a small puncture in the ball first.

2

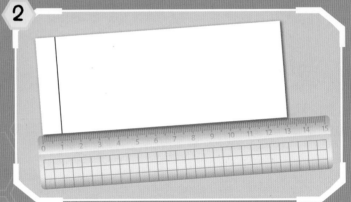

Cut out a 5 inch x 2 inch (13 cm x 5 cm) strip of thin cardstock. Down one end of the cardstock, draw a 0.5 inch (1 cm) line.

3

Draw a body and face on the front of the cardstock. You may want to decorate the clothing with a fun design.

4

Add glue to the cardstock, before the 0.5 inch (1 cm) line. Roll the strip of cardstock into a cylinder with the glued end overlapping, sticking it together so that it holds its shape.

5

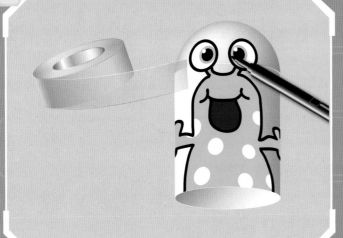

Tape one end of the cylinder to one half of the table tennis ball. Use the colored pens to finish up the drawing of the head.

6

Put a lump of modeling clay into the base of the other half of the table tennis ball. Now use the tape to stick it to the other half of the cylinder.

7

Now you are ready to stand your character upright. Try pushing it over, so that it stays horizontal. What happens?

What Happens?

The wobbling toy has a very low center of gravity because its top half is light, but the base is heavy. When you give it a push, gravity will pull it back to a point directly above the point where its mass is concentrated. This is called its state of equilibrium. Traffic cones also have a low center of gravity, with a wide heavy base to ensure they don't fall over.

BALANCING BUTTERFLY

You will need
- Thin cardstock
- A pencil
- Colored pens or paints
- Scissors
- 4 small coins
- Tape or superglue

Want to balance a piece of paper on your finger? Here's how, with a beautiful, balancing butterfly.

1

Draw a butterfly shape on a piece of cardstock. Make the wing tips higher than the head. It can look as realistic as you like.

2

Decorate the butterfly with colored pens or paints. Choose whichever colors you like.

3

Cut out the butterfly with scissors, working your way around the outline. Repeat steps 1 to 3 for a second butterfly.

4

Using superglue or tape, stick the coins to the wing tips of the two butterflies. Make sure they are secure.

5

Bend the wing tips of the first butterfly down a little bit. Then repeat this step with the second butterfly.

6

Balance the top of a butterfly's body on the tip of your finger. Does it hang evenly?

7

You can balance your butterfly pretty much anywhere! Add the two butterflies to the leaves of a sturdy house or garden plant.

What Happens?

When coin weights are added to a butterfly, the center of gravity falls directly between them, where your finger is, making it easy to balance the wings. Tightrope walkers use the same trick. They often carry a long flexible pole, with weights at either end. This lowers their center of gravity making it easier to balance.

PERISCOPE

Submarines use periscopes so that the crew can see above the waves while the submarine is underwater. They're also handy for seeing over the heads of crowds! Find out how a periscope works by building a simple version.

You will need

- An empty, clean fruit juice carton
- Glue • A ruler • Scissors
- 2 plastic mirrors— each 3 inches x 2 inches (7 cm x 5 cm)
- Packing tape
- Felt-tip pen

1

Remove the plastic spout on the carton. Seal the top down with packing tape.

2

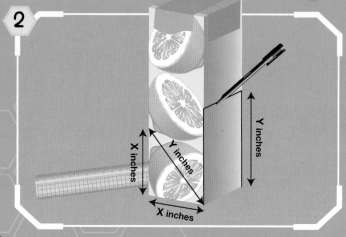

Measure the depth of the box (X) and mark the same distance up the side. Measure the diagonal (Y). Using the ruler, draw the outline of a square flap on the bottom of the front of the box. Use the same measurement (Y) for the flap's height and width.

3

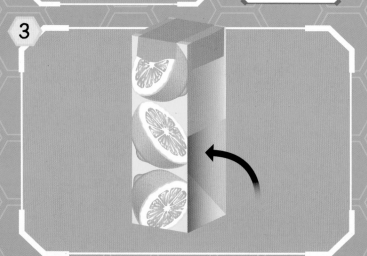

Cut three sides of the flap, and fold it inward to a 45° angle. Stick the flap in place with a piece of tape.

4

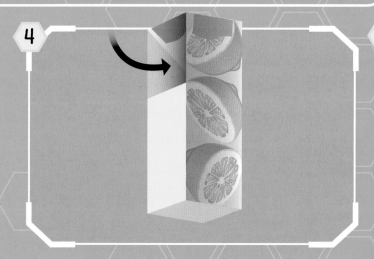

Repeat steps 2 and 3 at the other end of the carton, on the opposite side.

5

Glue a mirror to each of the slanted flaps.

Look through one end of the periscope. What can you see?

6

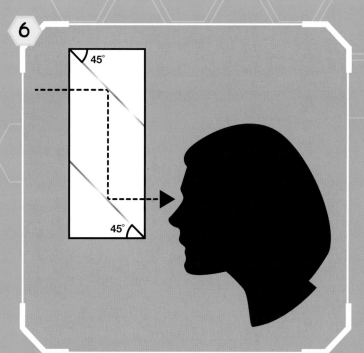

45°

45°

What Happens?

Light travels in straight lines. The first mirror changes the direction of the light by reflecting it. Then, the second mirror changes it back, parallel to its original path. Periscopes on submarines (above) allow the craft's navigator to check for ships and objects above the waterline, as well as the shore and the skies above.

ICE CREAM IN A BAG

This experiment will leave you with a tasty treat! Follow the steps to make ice cream in just ten minutes, thanks to the power of ice and salt.

You will need

- ½ cup (120 ml) whole milk or cream
- 1 tablespoon of sugar
- ½ teaspoon vanilla extract
- 2 small ziplock freezer bags
- 1 large ziplock freezer bag
- 4 cups of ice cubes
- A rolling pin
- A clean dishcloth
- 1 tablespoon of salt

1

In a small freezer bag, mix together the milk, sugar, and vanilla extract.

2

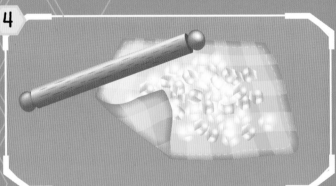

Push out as much air from the bag as possible, then seal the ziplock.

3

Place the first small freezer bag inside the second small freezer bag. Squeeze out the air, and seal it.

4

Fold the ice cubes into a dishcloth. Carefully bash the dishcloth with the rolling pin, crushing the ice cubes into small pieces.

5

Put the crushed ice cubes, together with a tablespoon of salt, into the large freezer bag.

6

Put the smaller bags inside the large freezer bag. Make sure the ice surrounds the small bags. Leave for ten minutes.

Place the contents of the small bag into a bowl. Now dig in to your delicious ice cream!

7

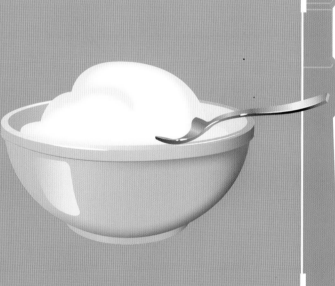

What Happens?

The salt lowers the freezing point of ice, so it melts faster. When it melts, it takes in heat energy from the surrounding environment—here, the ice cream mixture, which it cools down until it freezes. A hand-cranked ice cream maker (above) works in a similar way. Ice and salt are packed around a central bowl, and a crank churns the cream until it's frozen.

MARBLE MAGIC

You will need
- A wine glass
- A marble

Can any of your friends pick up a marble without touching it, then make it spin above the ground? Amaze them with some science magic!

1

You will need a bowl-shaped wine glass.

2

Challenge a friend to pick up a marble using the wine glass. He or she is not allowed to touch the marble or scoop it up.

3

Now show him or her how it's done. Place the glass directly over the marble.

4

Hold on to the base of the glass, and begin moving it in a circular motion. The marble should start rolling around inside the glass.

5

Speed up carefully. The marble will rise up to the widest part of the glass.

6

Keep rotating the glass, and carefully lift the glass with the marble off the ground.

What Happens?

This experiment is a contest between two forces: gravity and centrifugal force. As long as the marble is rolling fast enough, the centrifugal force pushing it outward to the widest part of the glass will be greater than the gravity pulling it downward. So the marble will roll around the glass rather then dropping out.

BATTLING BOOKS

You will need
- Two thick books, such as large catalogs or phone books
- Two volunteers

This experiment has books battling to hold on to each other as your friends try to pull them apart. It's all about the power of friction!

1

Take your two big books with plenty of pages. Phone books are ideal as the pages are floppy.

2

Place the front page of one book over the back page of the other. Now interleave the pages of the books, with the paper overlapping by a few inches.

3

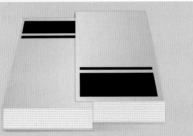

Continue placing the pages over each other until the books are completely combined.

4

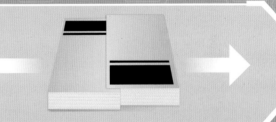

Now find two volunteers, and ask them to pull the books apart. It's a lot harder than it looks—in fact, it's impossible!

What Happens?

When you slide two pages across each other, a force called friction resists the movement. When all the pages of a book are overlapped, as in this experiment, that friction is multiplied by the number of pages. That's a lot of friction—so it's actually impossible for even the strongest person to pull the books apart!

KALEIDOSCOPE

Make your own kaleidoscope, and see thousands of crazy and colorful patterns.

You will need

- A paper towel tube
- A compass for drawing circles
- Paper • A pen
- Thin black cardstock
- Mirrored cardstock

- Small pieces of colored cellophane
- Colored wrapping paper
- A ruler • Scissors
- Tape
- Plastic wrap
- Tracing paper

1

Draw around the end of the paper towel tube onto a piece of paper.

Open your compass, and place its point onto the line of the circle, with the pencil placed in the middle of the circle. Draw the shape shown with dotted lines. Next, draw in the baseline of the triangle. Open your compass to this line, then mark in the third point of your triangle. Draw the complete triangle shape.

2

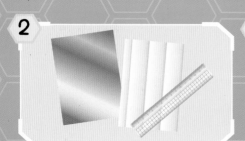

Draw a rectangle on the back of the mirrored cardstock, the same length as the tube, and cut it out. Mark out three parts the same width as the triangle base drawn in step 1.

3

Fold the mirrored cardstock along the marked lines, so that it becomes a triangular tube. The mirrored side should be on the inside. Slide it into the paper towel tube.

4

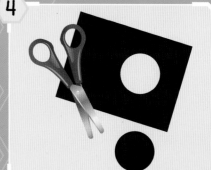

Draw around the end of the tube onto a piece of black cardstock. Cut out the circle.

5

Use tape to stick the black circle to one end of the tube. Use the end of the compass to make a hole in the center of the black cardstock.

6

Stretch some plastic wrap over the other end of the tube. Stick it in place with tape.

7

Cut a 1 inch (2.5 cm) wide strip of thin cardstock, and tape it around the end of the tube. Make sure it stands out a little from the end of the tube.

8

Scatter the small cellophane shapes onto the top of the plastic wrap end of the tube.

9

Draw around the bottom of the tube onto tracing paper. Use the compass to draw an outer circle, 0.5 inch (1 cm) larger than the original circle. Cut small flaps to the line of the inner circle. Place them over the plastic wrap end of the tube, and stick the flaps down with tape. Decorate the tube with wrapping paper.

10

You've made a kaleidoscope! Hold the plastic wrap end up to the light, look through the pinhole, and turn the tube. What do you see?

What Happens?

Light travels in a straight line. When it hits a mirror, it bounces off it in a different direction—this is called reflection. In a kaleidoscope, the light bounces around back and forth off the mirrored walls, creating multiple reflections of the colorful objects inside.

SOUNDS OF MUSIC

You will need
- Several similar glass bottles
- Water
- Stick or ruler
- Food color (optional)

Sound is produced in lots of ways. Just think of all the different types of musical instruments there are! Try a sound test that may inspire you.

1

Fill the bottles with different amounts of water. Place them in a row, starting with the most to the least water. Add a few drops of food color to vary the color of the water in each bottle.

2

Tap the bottles gently with a stick or ruler. Strike each bottle in the same place. What differences in sound do you notice?

3

Next, blow across the tops of the bottles, one by one. Try and get a clear note out of each one. How does the sound change from bottle to bottle?

What Happens?

Sound is made by creating vibrations in a material. These vibrations are carried through the air to our ears as sound waves. When each bottle is tapped, the glass bottle and the water inside vibrate. The more water there is in the bottle, the lower the pitch; the less water, the higher the pitch.

By blowing across the top of each bottle, sound is made by the vibrating volume of air inside each bottle. Here, the greater volume of air gives out a lower pitch, and the smaller volume of air gives a higher pitch. This is the exact opposite result to what happens when you tap the bottles with a stick.

JET POWER

Ever wondered how a jet engine works—or what makes a rocket blast off into space? This experiment will show you how a pushing force can power rockets to the Moon!

You will need

- A sausage-shaped balloon
- A plastic straw
- A piece of string about 23 feet (7 m) long
- A binder clip
- Tape

1

Thread the string through the plastic straw.

2

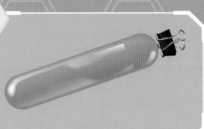

Fill the balloon with air, then put the binder clip on the neck to keep the air in.

3

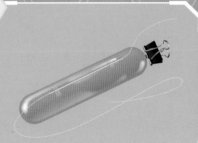

Tape the straw onto the balloon.

4

Tie each end of the string to a fixed object at least 20 feet (6 m) apart.

5

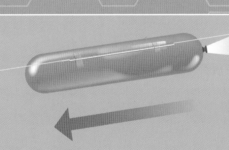

Count down to takeoff, and release the binder clip ...

... 5, 4, 3, 2, 1!

What Happens?

The air inside the balloon is under pressure. This is caused by the balloon trying to go back to its original shape. When the clip is released, air escapes through the neck, and the balloon is pushed in the opposite direction. This pushing force—called propulsion—thrusts the balloon forward. Jet engines and rockets work using a similar principle.

MAKE A ZOETROPE

Have you ever dreamed of being an animator? You can start right now by creating your first-ever moving picture, using just a few simple materials!

You will need

- A circular box with a lid
- Modeling clay
- Tape • A ruler • Scissors
- A thumbtack • A pen or pencil
- A small button
- A piece of cork
- Colored pencils or pens
- Black and white paper

1

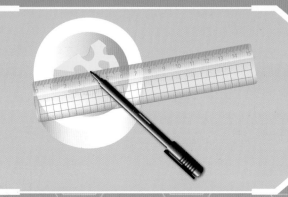

Using the ruler, find the exact center of the circular box and its lid. Make a small hole in the center of the box and lid with the thumbtack.

2

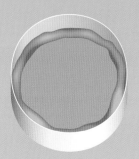

Put some modeling clay around the inside edge of the box.

3

Push the thumbtack through the middle of the lid, through the hole in the button, through the base of the box, and into a piece of cork.

4

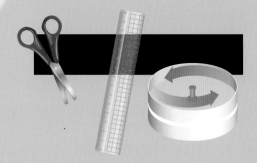

Cut a strip of black paper about 2.5 inches (6.5 cm) high. This will fit along the inside of the lid.

5

Draw lines along the back of the black paper about 1 inch (3 cm) apart. Cut slots down these lines about 1.5 inches (4 cm) deep.

6

Fix the black cardstock in place with tape. Then cut out a piece of white paper, about 1 inch (3 cm) wide, to fit inside it.

7

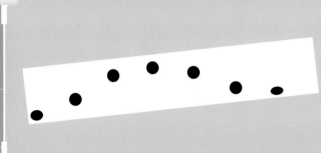

Draw in lines along the white paper, about 1 inch (3 cm) apart. This marks out your "frames." Draw a series of pictures in the frames.

8

Stick the strip with your drawings to the inside of the lid. Now spin the top, and watch your animation through the slits!

What Happens?

When you spin the zoetrope, you can see each of the pictures, one at a time in quick succession. Your brain tries to make sense of what your eyes take in. It interprets these rapidly changing pictures as movement, so that you see a continuous moving picture. This is how the first animations were made in the nineteenth century, before film was invented!

PAPER POPPER

You will need

- A sheet of paper 16 inches x 12 inches (40 cm x 30 cm)

Prepare to make a loud sound—with just one piece of paper! Folded correctly, this paper popper will give out a sharp bang.

1

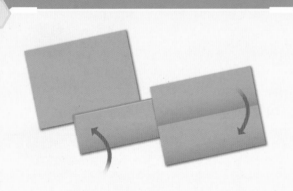

Fold the piece of paper in half lengthwise, then open it out. You could use white or colored paper, as long as it folds easily.

2

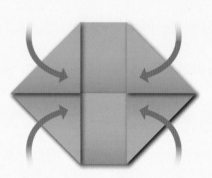

Fold down the four corners of the paper to the crease line in the middle.

3

Carefully fold the paper together along the first crease you made.

4

Fold the shape in half, with the pointed ends together. Make sure the points match up.

5

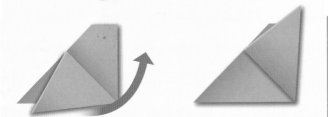

Make a triangular shape by folding back the bottom left pointed corner.

6

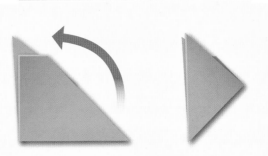

Turn the shape over, and make a matching fold on the other side.

7

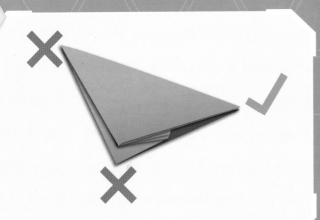

Turn your shape around until it looks like this. Hold the paper in the corner, where the green check is in the diagram above.

8

Now swing the paper popper downward as fast and as hard as you can. What can you hear?

What Happens?

Swinging the paper popper downward compresses (squashes) the air inside it. The air is suddenly freed when the inner fold opens out. This causes a rapid decompression—a small explosion of air that gives out a loud bang! Can you think of any other object that follows the same principle? What happens when you puncture a balloon?

ICE CUBE TRICK

You will need
- A glass
- Ice cubes
- Water • Salt
- Short piece of thread

Can you lift an ice cube out a glass of water without getting your hands wet or using a spoon? Yes, you can! Find out how, when you perform this simple experiment.

1

Put a big ice cube in a glass of water.

2

Pour a small amount of salt on the ice cube.

3

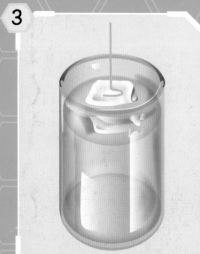

Dangle a piece of thread, so that it touches the salty patch on the ice cube. Hold it there for a few minutes.

4

Now, pull the thread upward, lifting the ice cube out of the glass.

What Happens?

The salt melts the top of the ice cube, but it eventually refreezes, causing the ice cube to stick to the end of the thread. This experiment works by using the melting and freezing properties of water and shows a principle called adherence. Adherence is when two objects attach to each other, as when the string attaches to the ice cube, making it easy to lift out of the glass.

BALLOON BUDDIES

In this experiment, you can create an electrostatic charge—a force that will cause two balloon buddies to ignore each other.

You will need
- 2 balloons
- A permanent marker
- String
- A wool sweater

1

Fill two balloons with air, and tie their necks. Attach string.

2

Bring your balloon buddies to life by drawing a face on each balloon with the permanent marker.

3

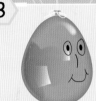

With the string, hang the balloon buddies up about 2 inches (5 cm) apart, and see where they settle.

4

Rub the faces of the balloons with a wool sweater.

5

Let the balloons hang freely on the strings. How do they behave?

What Happens?

In Step 3, the balloons settle with the faces pointing in any direction. In Step 5, the faces turn away from each other. Rubbing a balloon with woolen fabric produces an electrostatic charge on it. A similar charge on both balloons means that they will repel each other. The force should be strongest where the rubbing occurred, and so the faces turn away from each other.

GLOSSARY

Acid A chemical compound which is soluble in water, tastes sour, and neutralizes bases.

Adherence The property of sticking together.

Atom The smallest possible particle of a chemical element.

Base A substance that reacts to acids and neutralizes them.

Carbon dioxide (CO_2) A waste gas produced by the body, made up of one carbon atom bonded to two oxygen atoms.

Cellulose A substance that is the chief part of the cell walls of plants, and is used in making products such as paper and rayon.

Center of gravity The point that marks the center of an object's mass, so that it acts as a balancing point.

Centrifugal force The outward force felt by an object moving in a curved path around a central point.

Crystal A special kind of solid where the molecules are organised in a repeating pattern.

Emulsion A mixture of two liquids that would not normally mix. An emulsion contains tiny particles of one liquid suspended in another.

Freezing point The temperature at which a liquid becomes solid.

Friction The resistance of motion when one objects rubs against another. Friction slows moving objects.

Gas A substance that is like air and has no fixed shape.

Gravity A force which tries to pull two objects together. Earth's gravity is what keeps us on the ground, and what makes objects fall.

Liquid A substance with the consistency of water.

Molecule A group of atoms bonded together to form what is known a chemical compound.

Propulsion The force that moves something forward.

Saturated A solution that cannot absorb any more of a solute (the substance that is being dissolved).

Solid A substance that keeps its size and shape.

Static electricity Electricity that collects on the surface of something (giving it an electrostatic charge) and does not flow as a current. It can give you a mild shock if you touch an electrostatically charged surface!

Surface tension The force that pushes the molecules on the surface of a liquid together, making a layer.